I'm a Christian: What's Next?

I'm a Christian: What's Next?

ISBN-978-0-9762140-5-2

Artwork by Caswell Huff
Cover by Rob Baker
Layout by Moisés Pinedo

Printed in China

Peaceful House Publishing
3617 N. Georgetown Drive
Montgomery, Alabama
36109

Dedication

To my son Silas Reed Butt, whose innocence and smiling face remind me that truly the Kingdom of Heaven is composed of such childlike purity (Luke 18:16).

Acknowledgement

Special thanks to John Farber who contributed the first chapter to this book, and who sparked the idea for and co-wrote *Am I Ready to Be Baptized*, the first book in this two-book series.

Table of Contents

Note to Parents

Watching your child be baptized into Christ one of the most amazing things that a Christian parent can experience this side of eternity. Yet the wise mother or father understands that becoming a Christian is the beginning of a maturing child's Christian journey, certainly not the end. Each new babe in Christ needs nurturing and continued teaching from God's Word. New Christians need to be impressed with their new responsibilities, blessings, and promised rewards. They need to be equipped with the proper spiritual tools to deal with temptation, and to know how to handle it when they do occasionally sin.

It is often the case that parents of new Christian wonder where to start. What aspects of the Christian life need to be addressed first? What Bible stories, facts, and principles will help a young Christian get moving in the proper direction? This book was written to answer some of those very important questions. It is designed to show new Christians God's will about how they should worship, relate to their peers and their parents, and live godly lives. When a young person becomes a Christian, those close to him or her often wonder how they can help the new convert mature in Christ. By putting the babe in Christ in contact with the teachings in this book, a caring family member can help the new Christian respond to the question, "I'm a Christian: What's Next?"

Chapter 1

Starting the Race

Chris was so excited! Months of training with his dad had finally paid off. They were standing in a crowd of about 8,000 people getting ready to run their first marathon. They weren't there to try to win the race. They just wanted to finish. Not everyone has the guts to run 26 miles without stopping. In his mind, just finishing was going to be a major accomplishment in life.

People were everywhere. Some were stretching while others were bouncing on the balls of their feet to warm up their leg muscles. Most people were talking to others around them, but some were not talking at all. They were focused on the event ahead of them with their "game faces" on. One thing was for sure, it was a very energetic crowd. Everybody was watching the countdown clock at the front of the line, anxious for the race to get started.

Chris noticed all kinds of different people. He expected to be the youngest person, but there were lots of kids ready to run with their parents. There was a group of Marines dressed in dark brown shirts and shorts. They were lined up perfectly—four men across and eight men deep. One of them was in the very front holding an American flag. They were not talking. Some people were wearing sunglasses and listening to their iPods. Others were setting their watches to keep track of their pace throughout the

race. He even saw a group of men in wheel chairs!

Chris noticed an older gentleman a few feet from where they were standing. He looked older than Chris's grandparents. He certainly didn't look like he could run 26 miles without stopping. Chris caught himself staring at the old man, and turned away, but not before the two made eye contact.

Then, about two minutes before the race started, the old man leaned over to Chris. With a smile he said, "Keep your head down for the first mile." Chris was a little confused. He had been told by a lot of coaches in different sports to keep his head down. In soccer, keep your head down when trying to shoot a goal. In baseball, keep your head down to field a ground ball. In football, keep your head down when you run the ball. He didn't see the advantage of running with your head down for the first mile. He was curious so he asked, "Why?"

"This is my 25th marathon," said the old man, "And I've learned a few things along the way. There are about 8,000 people here trying to fit onto the same street to run in the same direction. Most injuries happen in the first mile. There are two reasons to keep your head down. Some want to run fast, and others want to run slow, but until people have a chance to spread out, you might trip over someone else's feet. Second, with so many people it's hard to see in front of you. If there is a pot hole in the ground, you could step in it and get hurt. You'll never see mile 26 if you can't make it past the first mile."

Chris looked up at his dad, who had heard everything the man said, then he turned back to the older man, "Wow! That makes a lot of sense. Thanks for the advice."

You see, it's almost impossible to finish a race if you get hurt at the beginning. That's why you see so many people stretching their muscles and warming up before they run. They want to stay in the race without getting injured.

You Are Running a Race—The Christian Race

The Bible calls the Christian life a race. The Bible tells us that we must "run with endurance [without quitting] the race that is set before us" (Hebrews 12:1). This book is designed to help you prepare to finish the Christian race that you started when you were baptized into Christ.

Just like the marathon that Chris and his dad were running, the race you have begun may be long, and finishing can be difficult. And just like the marathon, it is important to pay attention to how you start.

To get a good start, you need to understand that being a Christian is about purity. After all, when you were baptized, you were purified from sins. But what does it mean to be pure? Being pure simply means being "one thing." Scientifically it means that there is only one element. If you have a bar of pure gold, you can know there is no dirt or other element in the bar besides gold. It is very difficult to get a pure element, which is one reason pure gold is so expensive.

So what does it mean to be pure? For people to be pure they must be "one thing." For a Christian to be pure, the "one thing" one must focus on is Jesus Christ. Jesus is our "one thing." Some people say it like this, "Jesus must come first in your life." While that is a good way to think, it falls a little short. To be truly pure, not only should Jesus come first in your life, there shouldn't really be any competition. The Bible says in Colossians 1:16 that "all things were created through Him (Jesus Christ) and for Him." We are created for Jesus. He is our "one thing."

Galatians 3:27 says, "For as many of you as were baptized into Christ have put on Christ." Think of Jesus as a new

set of school clothes. If He is our "one thing," then Christ is the only "set of clothes" in the closet. We don't have an attitude that we "put on" for ballgames and take off for worship. We don't have a negative way to behave that we "put on" when we are around the "cool" crowd and take off when grown-ups are present. We simply "put on" our Christian attitude everywhere, all the time—at ballgames, around our friends, and in our homes. If Jesus is the only thing in your closet, then the whole world will be able to see that Christ is your focus everywhere you go.

Now that you are a Christian it will be important to keep yourself as pure as possible. As you read this book, you will learn many different ways to be a pure Christian. As you learn to be pure and focused on Jesus, you will be like a bar of gold, precious and valuable in the Lord's Kingdom.

Chapter 2

The Most Important Thing

Andrew loved Saturday mornings. He and a bunch of guys from the neighborhood would meet in Caleb's huge backyard to play football. Almost every Saturday for the past 8 months, Andrew laced his shoes up tight, grabbed his football, snatched a Pop Tart©, and rushed out the door. This Saturday was especially exciting. A new kid had moved into the neighborhood, and from what the other guys were saying, he could really play. He couldn't wait to see just how tough this new kid was.

Caleb's yard was about a 10-minute jog from Andrew's house. When he reached "the field" most of the boys were already warming up and stretching. They were waiting on Andrew. The gang counted on Andrew every Saturday to bring the most important part of the game. "Hey, Andrew. Great to see ya," Caleb yelled across the yard. "Glad you're here," blurted Tommy. "Hey, Drew, hook us up with the ball." Then it hit Andrew; he had forgotten the ball, the most important part of the whole game. He had left it sitting on his dresser at home. None of the other kids had a football and there was no way they could play without one. In all his excitement, he had forgotten the most important thing.

If you are reading this book, it means you probably are a young Christian. The choice you made to be baptized was the most important decision of your life. Your new Christian life is exciting and will be filled with all kinds of wonderful things. You will learn new things from God's Word that will help you grow. You will probably go to summer camps and youth events where you will meet other Christians and make friendships that will last many years. You will begin to respect and admire Christian men and women like your preacher, youth minister, and parents. But in all the excitement of being a new Christian, you must make sure that you do not forget the most important thing....

What is the most important thing about being a Christian? Is reading your Bible the most important thing? Is keeping your mind pure from bad thoughts the thing that ranks the highest? What about avoiding stealing, jealousy, or envy—is that the greatest goal of Christianity? While those things are very important, they are not the most important. To find out the most important part of being a Christian, we need to listen to what Jesus said.

The Bible tells a story about a man who came to test Jesus by asking Him a hard question. The man asked Jesus which commandment in the law was the greatest. Of course, the man probably thought all the commandments were important, and Jesus would not be able to give one that was the greatest. But Jesus answered the man by saying: "You shall love the Lord your God with all your heart, with all your soul, and with all your mind. This is the first and great commandment" (Matthew 22:36-37).

There it is, the greatest thing that you, as a new Christian, can do—love God with everything you have.

How Do I Love God?

Sometimes words like "love" are difficult to understand. What does it mean to "love" God? You can't give God a hug. You can't send God a card that tells how much you care for Him like you might send to your parents or brother or sister. So how do you "love" God? Thankfully, the Bible has told us exactly what "loving" God means. In John 14:15, Jesus said "If you love Me, you will keep My commandments." Loving God means doing what God has said. Some people claim to love God with all their hearts, but they do not obey God's commands found in the Bible. In truth, no matter what a person says, he can't love God unless he **does** God's will.

The Tragic Story of Saul

One man in the Old Testament is a great example of a person who claimed to "love" God, but did not do what God asked him to do. God told King Saul to

go and destroy the wicked Amalekites. Saul was also commanded to kill all the animals and livestock and bring nothing back. Saul went on the mission and did what God had said—almost. He destroyed all the worthless cattle, but saved many of the best sheep and oxen. The prophet Samuel approached Saul as he returned from the battle and asked Saul why he had disobeyed God. Saul said he saved the livestock so that the people could sacrifice them to God. He claimed to be "loving" God by bringing these animals to give to God. But Saul misunderstood what "loving" God meant. Samuel explained that God desires obedience more than sacrifice or any other gift that a person could give. God wants His children to obey Him. This is what loving God means—obedience.

Maybe you have seen children act like Saul. Sometimes a mother or father will tell a young child not to get a cookie out of the cookie jar. The parent might leave the room and the child sneaks over to the jar. Just as the child pulls her hand out of the jar, the parent comes back into the room catching her in the act of disobeying. What does the child do? The little girl might give the cookie to her

mommy or daddy and say, "I was just getting the cookie for you." Whether the child really wanted to give the cookie to the parent (which is most likely **not** the case) makes no real difference. The child had been told not to get a cookie and obedience is better than the "gift" of a cookie.

One day a young preacher saw a group of rowdy teenagers. He wanted to teach them something about God, so he approached them and began a

conversation with them. In a few minutes, the teenagers began to use curse words and tell some very dirty jokes. The young preacher reminded them that they were going to answer to God for all the things that they were saying and doing. One of the teenagers spoke up and said, "We know about God. He knows we love Him." Did those teens really love God? They might have said that they loved God, but their disobedient actions showed that they did not love Him.

Jesus Christ is the greatest example of love for God that has ever been given. In fact, Jesus said that He always did exactly what God wanted Him to do (John 8:29)—even when it came to dying on the cross. Jesus didn't really want to suffer the pain of dying on the cross. But He prayed that God's will would be done and not His own. Jesus truly loved God the Father with everything He had. The most important thing you can do as a new Christian is to decide right now that you will love God with all your heart, soul, and mind. By deciding to love God, you are deciding to do what He asks you to do.

And one more thing. If you go to play backyard football on Saturday mornings, make sure somebody brings the most important thing—the football.

Chapter 3

Being Kind to Others

Try to think about Jesus being a boy about twelve years old. What if you heard that the boy Jesus was going to visit your city? Not only that, He was coming to visit your house, and spend the day with you. How would you treat Him when He came to your door? Would you be kind to Him? Would you share your best video games, toys,

or bike? I'm sure if Jesus came to your house you would do everything you could to make sure that He had a wonderful time. You probably think that Jesus will never come to your house as a twelve year old to spend the day riding your best bike or playing with your latest toys. But did you know that Jesus **will** come to visit you? Let me explain.

When Jesus was on Earth, He told people what is going to happen at the end of time. He said that at the end of time, all people who ever lived will stand before Him to be judged according to what they did while they were on Earth. Jesus said that all the people will be divided into two groups—the sheep and

the goats. He said the sheep are those who will be on His right side and will get to go to heaven. The goats will be on the left side and they will be lost forever. Jesus also said that the people who did right will wonder why they get to be in heaven. They will want to know what they did to get to go to heaven. Jesus will answer the good people and say:

"When I was hungry, you fed me. When I was thirsty, you gave me something to drink. When I was sick and in prison, you came to visit me." The good people will be confused; they won't remember ever seeing Jesus. They will say to Him, "Lord, when did we see you hungry or thirsty, sick or in prison?" Jesus will answer them and say, "Whenever you did it to one of the least of the people, you did it for me."

What did Jesus mean? He meant that when a Christian helps a poor person, or someone who is hungry or thirsty, it is like they are helping Jesus. By showing love for other people, Christians show love for Jesus at the same time.

Then Jesus will turn to the wicked people on His left and say to them: "When I was hungry, you did not feed me. When I was thirsty, you did not give me anything to drink. When I was sick and in prison, you did not come and visit me." Now the wicked people will be very confused. As they look at Jesus, they will not remember seeing

Him on Earth. They never saw Him knock on their door and ask for food. And they knew they had never seen Him in prison. They will ask Him: "Lord, when did we see you hungry or thirsty? When did we see you sick or in prison?" Then Jesus will answer them: "Whenever you did not help the least person, you did not help Me." What did Jesus mean? He meant that the wicked people had seen many hungry, thirsty, and sick people in their lives, but they did not help them. By refusing to help those people, they were not helping Jesus. (For the full story read Matthew 25:31-46.)

You see, Jesus Himself will never come to your house to spend the day with you. But other young people will. Some may not have as many nice things as you have. Some may come from families that don't have as much food or as much money as your family. The way that you treat those boys and girls is the way that you are treating Jesus. That is a very important thing to know.

Think about being at school. Have you ever made fun of another kid and called him or her a bad name so that you could fit in with the "cool" group? Did you realize that when you called that kid a bad name, it was like you were calling Jesus a bad name? Have you ever invited the "cool" kids to your birthday party, but left out the one or two kids that nobody liked? Did you know that by not inviting them, it was like you did not invited Jesus?

However, this idea works both ways. Have you ever helped one of your classmates learn something in math or some other subject that was giving

them trouble? If you did, it was like you helped Jesus. Have you ever told other people at school to stop making fun of someone? When you did, it was like you were defending Jesus. How we treat other people is how we treat Jesus.

Who is Your Neighbor?

Jesus said the most important commandment is to love God with all your heart, soul, and mind. But Jesus said the second most important commandment is to love your neighbors as yourself. The man questioning Jesus then asked Him what He meant by the word "neighbor." To answer him, Jesus told the story of the Good Samaritan.

One day a man was walking down a road. Robbers attacked him, beat him, stole all his money and left him for dead.

He was hurt very badly and could not move. Soon, a priest came down the road. He saw the hurt man lying on the road. But instead of stopping to help, he walked by on the other side. A little while later, a worker in the temple came down the road. Surely he would help the man. But he did not help the wounded man. He walked right by just like the priest. Finally, a Samaritan came by. The Jews did not like Samaritans. But this Samaritan saw the wounded man. He stopped to help him, bandaged his wounds, and took him to a safe place. He paid lots of money so the man could have a safe place to rest and get well.

After Jesus told this story, he asked a question. He said: "Who was the neighbor to the man who was hurt?" The man listening to the story said that the Samaritan who helped the wounded man was his neighbor. Jesus said, "You are right." He then told the man to go and do kind things for others just as the Samaritan had done. Did you realize that when the Samaritan helped the wounded man, it was like he was helping Jesus?

Christians are supposed to be kind and good to other people. Anyone who needs our help is our neighbor, and we are supposed to help them. When we help people in need, it is like we are helping Jesus.

Now that you are a Christian, it is your job to be kind to others and treat them like you would treat Jesus. It is your job to be a friend to kids who other people don't like. It is your job to help those who are having a hard time fitting in, or need help doing better in math or reading. Just think! One day, if you have been kind to other people, Jesus will let you be with Him in heaven forever. When you wonder why you get to be in heaven, He may say something like: "When I sat by myself at lunch, you came and sat with me. When other people made fun of me, you told them to stop. When I needed lunch money, you shared yours with me." When we help others, we are helping Jesus.

Chapter 4

Talking To God

Lisa couldn't wait to get home and tell her mother the great news. For the past three weeks, Lisa and her mother had been practicing spelling words. Lisa's mother would say, "Spell, 'Conversation.'" When Lisa spelled the word correctly, her mother would tell her she was doing great. When she would miss the word, her mother would say, "Try again. Think hard and spell...." Sometimes her mother had to tell her how to spell the word, but for the last few days, Lisa had been able to spell almost every word. Lisa and her mother spent hours and hours studying for the school spelling bee, and all their hard work and practice paid off. Lisa won the school spelling bee and was on her way to compete in the district. If she won the district, she would go to the state competition. Her teachers told her what a great job she had done in the school contest and wished her luck at district. Her friends congratulated her and told her how happy they were that she had done so well. The comments from her friends and teachers made Lisa feel great. But what Lisa wanted to do more than anything was tell her mother.

Lisa burst through the front door of her house. "Mom. Mom. Guess what! Guess what happened today!" Her mother was standing in the kitchen when she heard the door open. She put down the bowl she was holding, wiped her hands on a kitchen towel, and hurried to the door. "What, Lisa? What happened?" She could see the excitement in Lisa's eyes. "I won, Mom, I won the school spelling bee." Lisa's mom gave her a huge

hug. "That's wonderful dear. Now tell me all about it." Lisa and her mom sat on the couch while Lisa told her everything that had happened. She told her mom all about the winning word, who missed what, which word she almost misspelled, and all the wonderful things her teachers had told her. Lisa's mom listened closely to every word. Lisa thought to herself how good it felt to have someone who really loved her and sincerely wanted to hear about the things that happened in her life. Lisa knew that her mother loved her so much that she would listen as long as Lisa wanted to talk. And Lisa knew that her mother would be there to hear all the good things that happened to her, and would be there if she had worries or fears she needed to discuss. Lisa loved having someone to talk to about anything and everything.

Have you ever had something very exciting happen to you? Maybe you won a race, did great on a test, or received a prize. Do you remember wanting to tell someone all about it? Or maybe there was a time when something happened to you that was not fun or exciting. In fact, maybe it was something that was bad. Maybe you failed a test, got in a fight at school, or were not invited to a birthday party by someone you thought was your friend. Do you remember wanting to talk about it with someone you loved, like your mom or dad or best friend?

The truth is, there is Someone Who loves you more than anyone else in the world, and He always wants to hear about the things that make you happy or sad. That person is God. God made you and He loves you very much. He wants you to talk to Him when something great happens to you. And He wants you to tell Him when you are afraid, sad, or hurt. The wonderful thing about God is that you can talk to Him any time of day from

any place in the world. You don't have to be in a church building on Sunday morning. You can talk to God when you are on the pitcher's mound playing a baseball game or lying in your bed at night before going to sleep.

You might wonder how you can talk to God. You have probably heard the words "pray" or "prayer" before. When a person prays or says a prayer, that person is talking to God. The Bible says a lot about prayer. When we read about Jesus, we see that He prayed often. In Luke 5:16, the Bible says that Jesus went into the wilderness and prayed. In Luke 6:12, Jesus went out to a mountain and prayed to God all night long. Jesus loved to talk to God the Father. Just before Jesus was betrayed and crucified, He spent many hours in the Garden of Gethsemane praying to God. If we are trying to be like Jesus, which is the goal of every Christian, then we will follow His example and talk to God often.

How Should We Pray?

You may wonder how to pray. Should we always bow our heads and close our eyes? Should we always speak out loud, or can God understand us if we pray "inside" just thinking the words? Should we fold our hands? The truth is, there is not a certain way that you need to sit or a certain way to bow your head all the time. In the Bible, we read that some people knelt on their knees to pray (read Acts 20:36). Some people stood up to pray (read 1 Kings 8:22). Jesus fell on the ground in the Garden of Gethsemane to pray (read Mark 14:35). And Hannah, the mother of Samuel, prayed to God without speaking out loud, by praying "inside" and thinking about what she wanted to say to God (read 1 Samuel 1:13). The most important thing is not how you hold your hands or whether you bow your head. The most impor-

tant thing is that you really concentrate on talking to God and show honor and respect for God. Many of the Pharisees prayed to God in very loud voices to be seen by other people. Jesus said that God would not listen to their prayers because they were praying to be seen by men and not to be heard by God. Whenever you pray, make sure you are not bowing your head, closing your eyes, or folding your hands just so people will think you are "good" at praying. But remember to truly think about God and talk to Him.

What Should We Pray About?

Should you pray about getting a new bike? Should you pray for God to help you win a soccer game? Are there things you should not pray for? Are there things God wants you to talk to him about? The truth is, God wants you to talk to Him about what is on your mind. He says that you can "cast all your cares on Him because He cares for you" (1 Peter 5:7). That means that you can pray about anything. You can pray about your friends, your pets, your

ball games, your grades, your family, or anything else that you think about and care about. God also says that you can ask Him to help you defeat the temptations that the devil sends your way.

There is also one very important thing that God wants you to remember in your prayers. He wants you to remember to be thankful for all the good things He has given to you—like food, a place to live, friends and family, and the wonderful gift of His Son Jesus. In Philippians 4:6, the Bible says: "Be anxious for nothing, but in everything by prayer…, with thanksgiving, let your requests be made known to God." Thanksgiving, or being thankful, is a very important part of our prayers.

God loves you more than anyone else in the world loves you, and He wants you to talk to Him about whatever is on your mind. He is never asleep, never away on vacation, and never too busy to listen. You can tell Him anything at anytime, and He will be there to listen. God hears you, He loves you, and He will listen to your sincere prayers.

[The Bible says so much about prayer that this short chapter cannot cover everything. Here is a list of some more verses that will help you learn more about prayer:

Matthew 6:5-15

Mark 9:37-38

John 16:23-24

1 Timothy 2:1-4

James 5:16-18

1 John 5:14-15

1 Thessalonians 5:17]

Chapter 5

Feeding Our Souls

Alyssa's birthday had been terrific. Many of her friends, cousins, and family came to her party. They brought her all kinds of neat presents. She was given a new bike, some new school clothes, a gift-certificate or two, and lots of other stuff. Emily, one of her friends from school, gave her a small fish bowl and a new gold fish to live in it. For some reason, the gold fish and fish bowl were Alyssa's favorite present. She had never had a gold fish before, and she was looking forward to having the pretty fish and fish bowl in her room.

Everything was going fine for several days. The fish was healthy and swam happily in its watery home. But soon Alyssa's mom began to notice that the fish had stopped swimming so much. In fact, it spent most of its time sitting still on the bottom of the bowl near the little red rocks. As she continued to check on the fish over the next several days, it began to have trouble staying upright. Soon, the fish was floating upside down on top of the water, dead.

Alyssa's mom was the first to notice. When Alyssa came home from school, she told her the bad news. Then she asked her if she knew why the fish might have died. Suddenly, it hit Alyssa. For the past week or so, she had been so busy that she had forgotten to feed the fish. It died because she didn't give it the food that it needed to live. Alyssa learned a valuable lesson.

We can learn a valuable lesson from this story as well, but it's not about fish food. The lesson we need to learn is that without food, living things die. But did you know that all people need a special kind of food? They need food like meat and vegetables for their bodies, but they need something else, too. They need to feed their hearts and minds with the Word of God. If people do not read and study God's Word, then their souls die just like the fish died. The Bible says: "Man shall not live by bread alone, but by every word that proceeds from the mouth of God" (Matthew 4:4). That means that bread might keep a person's body alive, but God's Word is the food for a person's soul.

The Owner's Manual

There are lots of reasons why studying God's Word is important. God made you and He knows exactly what you need to do in order to be happy. Have you ever had a new toy like a remote control car, or an electronic gadget like a video game or MP3 player? Those toys and gadgets come with owner's manuals. An owner's manual is a small book that tells the owner how to use something. For instance, it tells what kind of batteries a toy uses, whether you can use the toy in water, how hot or cold the toy can get, and all kinds of other useful information. This information is very important. For instance, suppose you buy a remote control car that cannot work in water. If you don't know that, and try to run the car through deep mud puddles, the car will break and be useless.

In a similar way, the Bible is like an owner's manual for a person. God created us and knows exactly how we need to act in order to be happy. He

knows that we cannot be happy if we lie to others, so He tells us not to lie (read Ephesians 4:25). He knows that humans cannot live happy lives if they steal from each other, so He tells us not to steal (read Ephesians 4:28). Some people try to be happy without reading the Bible and following God's commandments, but they can't do it. In fact, the Bible says that when humans try to make up their own rules, they fail. The writer of the book of Proverbs said: "There is a way that seems right to a man, but its end is the way of death" (Proverbs 14:12). Since God created humans, only He knows enough about them to write the "owner's manual."

The Word Will Judge Us

Another reason studying the Bible is so important is because the words of the Bible will judge us at the end of our lives. When you take a test at school, what judges whether your answers on the test are right or wrong? Usually, the textbook is the judge of your answers. That means if your history book says that Christopher Columbus sailed in 1492, and you put on the test that he sailed in 1992, you miss the question. If you put that he sailed in 1492, like the textbook says, then you get it right. When you read the book, you find the information that judges you when you take the test.

Similar to a test at school, Jesus said His Word will judge us. Jesus said: "He who rejects Me, and does not receive My words, has that which judges him—the word that I have spoken will judge him in the last day" (John 12:48). The words that Jesus spoke are written in the New Testament. That means that the words of the New Testament will judge us. What does it mean that the words of Jesus will judge us? It means, if the Bible says we should not lie, we better not lie. If we continue to lie, then on the Day of Judgment, God will explain that the Bible said not to lie and we did it anyway. We will not pass the test. But what if our friends said it was alright to lie? Will that be a good enough reason for God to let us pass the test? No, because we are not judged on the word of our friends, but on God's Word. What if our preacher says it's okay to lie? Will God be happy with us if we lie? No, because we will not be judged by the word of our preacher. We will be judged on the words of the New Testament. That is why we must know what Jesus said in the New Testament, so that we can pass "the test" on the Day of Judgment.

Showing God We Love Him

Another reason we should read and study the Bible is because when we do, it shows that we love God. Jesus said: "If you love me, keep my commandments" (John 14:15). If we really love Jesus and are thankful for His sacrifice on the cross, we will want to keep His commandments. Those commandments are found in the Bible. When we read the Bible and do what it tells us to do, it shows that we love God. It is like your mother giving you a list of chores to do, and telling you that she really needs them done. If you love her and want to obey her, you will read the list and do the chores. If you don't read the list, you can't do the chores on the list, and it shows that you don't really love your mother like you should. When we learn God's Word and do what it says, we are saying to God that we love Him and are thankful for all that He has done for us.

When the apostle Paul wrote to the young preacher Timothy, he told him "to give attention to reading" (read 1 Timothy 4:13). He was telling Timothy to make sure He read the Bible often. You see, the Bible is the "road map" that shows us how to get to heaven. Just like a person cannot travel across the world without directions and a map, no one can get to heaven without the instructions found in the Bible. King David said that God's Word is like a lamp to our feet and a light to our path (Psalm 119:105). It shows us the way to live with God forever in heaven.

Remember, we need to know God's Word because it is like food for our soul. God gave it to us as the manual that shows us how to be happy. The Bible will be what judges us in the last day. When we study it, we show God that we love Him and care what He has to say to us. And only the Bible can tell us how to get to heaven. Let's remember to study it and do what it says so we can enjoy all the wonderful things God has planned for us!

Chapter 6

What Am I Going to Do Today?

Imagine having a magic piggy bank in your room. Every morning when you wake up, the bank is filled with $86,400. For as long as you can remember, this special bank has been filled every morning with piles of money. But the money has one very unusual quality. At the end of the day, whatever you did not spend vanishes into thin air. In the past, you tried to save some extra hundred-dollar bills under your pillow or in your dresser drawer, but every night the hidden money disappeared. You've talked to your friends about your bank and surprisingly, they all have banks exactly like yours.

The challenging thing about your bank is that each morning you must decide how to spend $86,400. You watch your friends to see how they spend theirs. Some of them buy thousands of dollars of junk. They buy candy, gum, soda, sweets, and things that are not good for them and are gone quickly. Others spend thousands of dollars doing fun things like riding go-karts, playing miniature golf, going to see movies (some even rent out the skating rink and bowling alley for all their friends). Others buy hundreds of books, computer programs, and educational stuff that helps them get smarter. And some of your friends buy phones, computers, and Internet access to keep in touch with their friends. One group of your friends simply acts like it is a pain to have so much money and they mope around doing nothing while their money

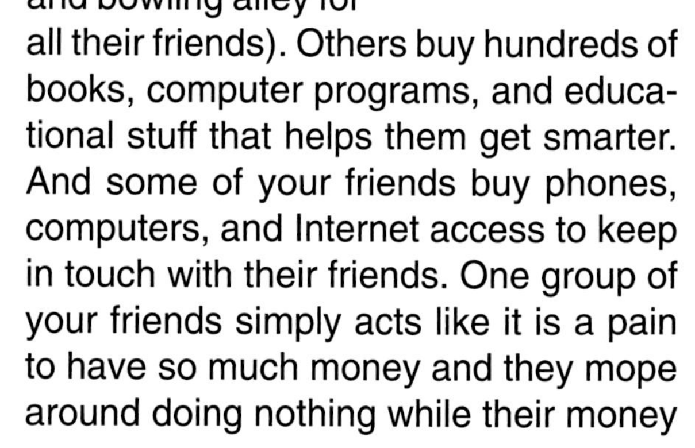

disappears each day. As you look at all your friends, you try to decide the best way to spend your $86,400.

In case you have not guessed yet, 86,400 is the exact number of seconds that are in each day. Every morning when you wake up, you must decide how you are going to spend each second and minute of your time. You might not have thought about it, but time is a very precious gift that God gives every person. In fact, God wants you to be very thoughtful and careful about how you use your time. In the book of Ephesians, the apostle Paul said: "See then that you walk carefully, not as fools but as wise redeeming the time, because the days are evil" (Ephesians 5:16). What does Paul mean by "redeeming the time?" He means that your time is valuable and should be used in ways that will bring glory to God. Let's look at several questions we should ask ourselves about how we spend our time.

Will This Help Me to Think about Good Things?

Even though there is nothing wrong with playing video games or watching television, some video games and TV programs contain things that Christians should not watch. Some video games suggest that it is cool to do drugs, hurt policemen, curse, and break the law. Some television programs show scenes of men and women doing things they shouldn't be doing. And the Internet often has sinful pictures of people who are showing too much of their bodies to the world.

One of the first things you should ask yourself is: Does the activity I have chosen help me think good thoughts or tempt me to think about things I should not? The Bible says: "Finally, brethren, whatever things are true, whatever things are noble, whatever things are just, whatever things are pure, whatever things are lovely, whatever things are of good report, if there is any virtue and if there is anything praiseworthy—meditate (or think) on these things" (Philippians 4:8). If a movie, TV program, video game, or Internet site tempts you to think about bad things instead of good things, then you should not waste your valuable time involved in it.

Am I Spending Too Much Time Doing This Activity?

People like to spend their time doing different things. Some like to hunt, fish, play sports, read, watch TV, hike, or all sorts of activities. In fact, there are thousands of activities that are safe, fun, and healthy. But sometimes these good activities can become bad activities if we do them too much. Think about a person who likes basketball. There is nothing wrong with basketball. It is a fun sport that can be healthy and safe. But what if a person loves basketball so much that he never studies for his school work because he is always shooting hoops? He won't help do chores at home because he is at the gym playing ball. And he never has time to read his Bible or go to youth group activities because he is always on the court. Even though basketball is a good activity, it can become bad if a person spends too much time doing it. Jesus once told about a group of people who let their desire for things of the world (like basketball) choke out their love for Him (read Mark 4:19). School work, sports, hunting, fishing, and reading fun books can all be great ways to spend some of your time. But you must make sure that you are not using too many of your 86,400 seconds on things that are not the **most important**.

Am I Making Time to Do What God Has Asked Me to Do?

There are certain things that God has asked each of us to do. Let's look at three things God has asked us to do. (The Bible mentions many more than three things we should be doing, but these are three good examples.)

Pray

In the Bible, God said that we should "pray without ceasing (or stopping)" (1 Thessalonians 5:17). This does not mean that we should pray every second of the day. It means that we should not go long periods of time like entire days, or weeks, or months, without talking to God. Just like we make time to talk to people we care about on a regular basis, we should make time to talk to our Heavenly Father as well.

Read the Bible

The Bible is the word of God. It is God talking to us. By reading and studying it, we learn exactly how God wants us to behave. The apostle Paul told Timothy to be diligent (study often) to show himself approved to God (2 Timothy 2:15). In fact, just like a baby drinks milk and grows bigger and gets stronger, the Bible helps new Christians grow stronger in their spiritual lives (1 Peter 2:2). In the same way we make sure that we eat lunch and supper almost every day, we should make sure that we eat the "spiritual food" of God's Word regularly.

Help Others

Many people are selfish and only look out for themselves. Christians should not be that way. The Bible says that we are to look out not only for our own needs but also for the needs of others (Philippians 2:3-4). That may mean taking time to help a fellow student with math when we would rather be talking on the phone to our friends, or taking time to write a card to a sick friend when we would rather be watching television. Helping others is very important because by helping them, we are showing that we love God.

Every day God gives you 86,400 very valuable pieces of time. And each day you must decide how you will use these precious gifts. One of the most important questions of your entire Christian life is: "What am I going to do today?"

Chapter 7

Important Words

John, Nikki, and James were camping out by themselves for the first time ever. Nikki and John were 14 and James had just turned 15. In the last few years, they had been camping with their dads and some other men and teenagers in the youth group at church. When James began to plan his 15th birthday party, he thought that a campout with his two best friends would be great. His parents said that if the boys would be extremely careful, and keep a cell phone close, then they could spend a night camping by themselves. James' dad had driven them to his family's property about 10 miles out of town and dropped them off for the night. He told them he'd come back the next morning. The three teens were a little nervous when he left, but they were excited about all the fun they expected to have.

After about an hour, the tent was up and ready. John had a campfire burning in the middle of camp that was circled by stones. James poked a hot dog onto a straightened-out metal clothes hanger and dangled it over the open flame. "This is the life, isn't it boys?" John and Nikki agreed. The three boys spent the next few hours talking about girls, which cars they wanted when they turned 16, and sports. As the hours slipped by, their eyes became heavy and they settled in their sleeping bags. John walked around the camp site one more time. "Don't you think this wood pile is a little too close to the fire, James?"

"Nah, that wood's too wet to burn. And the fire is almost out. There is just a little spark left. It won't hurt anything." James replied.

"Are you sure?" Nikki asked. "It looks a little close to me."

"It's not. Trust me. I've camped enough to know this stuff," James retorted as he crawled into his cozy sleeping bag. After a few more minutes of talk about school, the boys were sound asleep.

Suddenly, they woke with a start. Smoke was pouring into the tent. Their eyes burned and they began coughing. They rushed out of the tent and saw that the little spark in the fire had blown over into the wood pile and started a huge fire. Luckily, James had grabbed the cell on the way out of the tent. He quickly called his dad. Within twenty minutes, his dad was there with the fire truck close behind. Thankfully, the firemen put out the fire before it could spread to anyone else's field. The boys knew they were in trouble, and they knew it would be a long time before they were allowed to camp by themselves again. However, they did learn a valuable lesson—a little spark can start a big fire.

A Little Spark

The Bible tells us that the tongue is like a little spark. In James 3:5-6, the Bible says: "See how great a forest a little fire kindles! Even so the tongue is a fire." What is James telling us? He is saying that our words may seem little or unimportant, but they are really very powerful. What we say has the potential to do wonderful things and help others, but our words also have the potential to do great harm and destroy others. We must watch our words just as closely as we would watch a fire at a camp site. Let's look at some ways we must watch our words.

Lying

Telling the truth is one of the most important things in the world. The Bible says that God always tells the truth and He cannot lie. The Bible also says that the devil is the father of lies and he invented lying (read John 8:44). When a person lies, he is using a destructive tool that the devil designed to hurt others. The Bible says: "Therefore, putting away lying, let each one speak truth with his neighbor" (Ephesians 4:25). Many times in the Bible we read that we must tell the truth. But we know that telling the truth is not always easy. Sometimes, if we tell the truth, we will get punished or lose a privilege. Other times, telling the truth might cost us a friendship with someone at school. But the Bible

explains to us that Christians are people who tell the truth. In fact, in the book of Revelation, we read that "all liars" who do not repent will go to hell (Revelation 21:8). Even though telling the truth might cost us something now, it will be better for us later. God always rewards those who tell the truth.

Building Up Others

It is tempting to try to make yourself look good in front of your friends. One way that some people try to make themselves look good is by making someone else look or feel bad. These people make fun of others. They laugh at the kids in their class who have glasses or braces. They snicker and giggle when someone accidentally falls on the play-

ground. These bullies make fun of the clothes other kids wear, what other kids bring for lunch, and anything else they can think of. One reason they do this is because these bullies really feel bad about themselves. They are not happy, and they don't want others to be happy either, so they bring them down by making fun of them.

The Bible tells us that Christians should never try to bring others down by making fun of them. The Bible says we should try to build others up. The apostle Paul said: "Let no corrupt communication proceed out of your mouth, but what is **good** for necessary **edification**, that it may impart grace to the hearers" (Ephesians 4:29). The word "edification" means "building up." Paul is saying that we should only say those things that will help others and build them up, edify them, not bring them down. In the movie Bambi, a little rabbit named Thumper visits Bambi soon after he is born. Since Bambi is so young, he cannot walk very well and often falls. Thumper makes fun of Bambi, and Thumper's mother corrects him. He is told to recite the rule at their house. He says: "If you can't say something good, don't say anything at all." That is a great rule, and it is exactly what the Bible says. If you can't say something that will build others up, then you should not say anything at all.

Bragging or Boasting

We all want our friends to think we are cool, good at sports, smart, and generally good at stuff. One way some people try to accomplish this is by bragging or boasting. They talk about how much money their parents have, or how much their new bike cost. Sometimes they may talk about how fast they can run or how many goals they kicked at the last soccer game. But the Bible says

that boasting is not a good way to use our tongues. In fact, the Bible says that boasting is a sin like telling lies or even murder (Romans 1:29-30). Instead of boasting and bragging about how good we are, the Bible says we should give God glory and help others see how important **they** are to God. If we humble ourselves in this way, God tells us that He will be the one to lift us up before others (James 4:10).

Remember, your words are very powerful. You can use them to do good things by telling the truth, building others up, and glorifying God. Or you can choose to use them to do destructive things like lying, making fun of others, and bragging. As Christians, we must watch our words and make sure we use them for good. We must be careful to make sure they don't get out of control and destroy those around us.

Chapter 8

Worship

Ms. Johnson had been a Christian for over 70 years. She was the oldest member of the congregation. She was 86 years old, but she was still very active and very intelligent. She sat on the second pew toward the front on the right side of the church building. She had been sitting there as long as Emily could remember. Emily was 12. She had just been baptized a few weeks ago. She and her family sat three rows behind Ms. Johnson. And she had watched Ms. Johnson carefully for several weeks now.

As she watched her, she noticed several things. She noticed that she was always on time. She never came in late, always brought her Bible, and she sometimes brought visitors from the apartments where she lived. Emily also realized she was always there. Every Sunday morning, Sunday night, Wednesday night, and through all special meetings or Vacation Bible Schools. Emily noticed that she sang with every song, even with the new ones she didn't know so well. She watched as Ms. Johnson listened to the preacher, and followed along in her Bible when the preacher would mention Bible verses. Emily also saw that she bowed her head to pray, and would sometimes nod her head as if to say that she agreed with what was being said.

Today, Emily and her family arrived early for worship service. Emily sometimes visited Ms. Johnson before the service because she brought candy to give to the kids. Emily knew she was getting a little old to be one of the "kids" who came to Ms. Johnson for candy.

As she walked up to Ms. Johnson's pew, she turned to greet Emily.

"Hello Emily. Good to see you this morning," she said as she handed her some candy.

"Good to see you, too, Ms. Johnson. Thank you for the candy," Emily responded politely.

"Oh, you are so welcome. I've been wanting to talk with you, I heard that you just became a Christian. I think it was two weeks ago, wasn't it" Ms. Johnson asked.

"Yes, Ma'am. It was two weeks ago on a Monday night," Emily said as she opened a peppermint.

"Emily, do you know what one of my favorite things about being a Christian is?"

"What, Ms. Johnson?"

"Well, Emily, one of my favorite things about being a Christian is worship; what we do here on Sunday. You see, worship is a very special time for the Christian. It is the time when Christians present themselves to God." As she spoke, she had a hint of excitement in her eyes.

"I'm not sure I understand, Ms. Johnson, what do you mean 'present' ourselves to God?" asked Emily.

"I mean that God is in Heaven, and we can't go to Heaven and be with Him while we are on the Earth. But we can talk to Him through prayer, and sing to Him in songs, and be with Him in a spiritual sense."

"I'm still not sure I get it," said Emily as she tried to understand, "What do you mean a 'spiritual sense'?"

"Well, I mean that when you pray or sing to God, even though you can't see Him, He is listening to you. And when the whole congregation worships God by praying, or singing, or taking the Lord's Supper, it's like we're surrounding God's throne in Heaven. He hears us, and our songs, prayers, and thoughts make Him very happy."

"Oh, really?" said Emily. "I hadn't ever thought about worship that way. When you think about it like that, I guess worship is pretty important, isn't it?"

"Oh, yes, dear. It is one of the most important things in the world for a Christian to do. In fact, Jesus said, in John 4:24, that God is looking for people who will worship Him in spirit and in truth. Do you know what 'in spirit and in truth' means, Emily?"

"I'm not sure. I think, the words 'in truth' mean doing things the way God has said do them in the Bible. But I don't really know what 'in spirit' means."

"You're right, Emily, the words 'in truth' do mean worshiping as God has said. It means we pray in the name of Jesus, take the Lord's Supper on the first day of the week, sing with our voices, and give our money, just as the Bible teaches," Ms. Johnson said, as she handed a small red-headed boy some candy. She turned back to Emily and began to explain, "The words 'in spirit' mean that we concentrate on what we are doing. That means we think about God when we sing, we think about Jesus during the Lord's Supper, and we truly concentrate on what's being said during prayers. When we worship in spirit, we don't talk to our friends during the sermon, pass notes during the Lord's Supper, or think about school during the singing. We think about being in the presence of God; being around His throne."

Emily was really listening to Ms. Johnson now. She had tried to think about God during worship, but she often got distracted. Sometimes she even fell asleep during the sermon, and her mind would wander to TV shows during the prayer. Emily wondered if there was some "trick" to making sure her mind was concentrating on worship.

"Ms. Johnson," she said, "It seems kinda hard to always be thinking about the singing, praying, or sermon during worship. Is there something special I need to do to make it easier?"

"I can see you are growing up, Emily. Let me tell you, concentrating on worship is difficult. I have been trying to do it for 70 years and I'm still not perfect at it. But, I keep getting better. The important thing to remember is that God is watching. If you remember that, it will help you concentrate on what you are doing." As she spoke, the song leader began making his way to the front to start the service. Emily needed to get back to her seat. Before she left, she said, "Thanks, Ms. Johnson for the candy, and for helping me understand worship."

"You're welcome, dear. I'm glad you're a Christian. I hope we have many more Sundays to worship God together here on Earth. But I can't wait to gather around God's throne in Heaven and worship Him there for all eternity. Just remember, God loves it when we worship Him in spirit and truth. He is watching and listening."

As Emily started back to the pew where her family sat, she knew that something had changed. She knew that she needed to concentrate during worship, listen to the sermon, and think about Jesus during the Lord's Supper. Emily was growing up. She was a Christian now, and it was time that she focused on God and added her voice to the singing and her mind to worship.

Chapter 9

The Lord's Supper: Don't Forget to Remember

Bar-b-que ribs and chicken fill the hot Summer air with a delicious smell. Canned sodas covered with ice rest in a cooler on the porch just waiting for someone's hand to fish them out. A ripe red watermelon sits on the picnic table with a spoon in the center. Ahhh..., the Fourth of July, one of America's favorite outdoor holidays. And in the middle of all the bar-b-que, watermelon, and family get-togethers, one of the most exciting elements of the day has not even been mentioned—the fireworks.

In all the excitement, sometimes it is difficult to remember what the Fourth of July is really all about. If someone asked you why we celebrate the Fourth, could you tell him? Could you explain that on July fourth, 1776, our founding fathers signed the Declaration of Independence, which stated that the United States was separating from Great Britain? In fact, the Fourth of July has been set aside as a holiday in order for Americans to remember those founding fathers and how brave they were to declare their independence. Isn't it easy to forget why we do some things?

Now let's think about a Sunday morning service in the middle of the Summer just before you go on vacation. You are looking forward to a fun-filled trip to Florida. At worship this Sunday, the Lord's Supper comes directly after the sermon. The men stand up in front and bless the bread, pass it around, and it

comes to you. You pinch off a small piece, put it in your mouth and.... And what? What happens when you put that tiny little piece of unleavened bread in your mouth? Where does your mind go? Do you focus your mind on the purpose of the Lord's Supper, or do you forget the reason for the bread and grape juice?

The night before Jesus was betrayed, tried, and crucified, He ate the Passover feast with His twelve apostles. Often called the Last Supper, Jesus gathered with His apostles in the upper room and explained that He was soon to be betrayed. In the middle of this sad occasion, Jesus "took bread, blessed it and broke it, and gave it to the disciples and said, 'Take, eat; this is my body.' Then

He took the cup and gave thanks, and gave it to them saying, 'Drink from it, all of you. For this is My blood of the new covenant, which is shed for many for the remission of sins' " (Matthew 26:26-28). The gospel of Luke tells us that Jesus also told the apostles to "do this in remembrance of Me." Jesus' purpose for giving us the Lord's Supper was to give us a reminder of His sacrifice, death, and resurrection.

What Should We Eat and Drink?

Have you ever wondered why a "special" kind of bread called "unleavened bread" and grape juice are used for the Lord's Supper? Why don't Christians just use regular bread and water, or pizza crust and soda?

First, we need to know what the term "unleavened" means. Unleavened means that the bread does not rise like a loaf, but stays flat like a cracker. It means that there is no yeast or leaven in the bread. In the Old Testament, the

Jews could eat only unleavened bread during the Feast of the Passover. Since Jesus ate the Last Supper during the Feast of the Passover, He used unleavened bread. The reason we still use that kind of bread today is simply to follow the example of Jesus.

Why do we use grape juice for the Lord's Supper? That is simple. Jesus used grape juice. The phrase "fruit of the vine" in the Bible means grapes. And Matthew 26:29 says that Jesus used the juice from the "fruit of the vine" for the Last Supper. So, in order to follow the example of Jesus, we use unleavened bread and grape juice not pizza crust and soda.

On The First Day of the Week

As you talk to people in different religions, you will soon discover that many of them take the Lord's Supper only a few times a year, or once every month. Does the New Testament give us an example of how often we should take the Supper?

In Acts chapter 20:7, we read "Now on the first day of the week, when the disciples came together to break bread..." The phrase "to break bread" is used in this verse to refer to the Lord's Supper. This verse explains that the purpose for the Christians coming together was "to break bread." The Lord's Supper was the main reason they came together on the first day of the week. Which "first day of the week" was this? Was it the first one of the month, a special Christmas service, or a bi-monthly get-together?

In the book of 1 Corinthians, Paul is answering several questions regarding things that were happening in worship at the church in Corinth. One of those things that needed to be addressed was the Lord's Supper; another was the way that the church was giving their money. In 1 Corinthians 16:2, Paul explained that the church needed to do their giving "on the first day of the week." The Bible shows that the Christians met every first day of the week. The purpose of that meeting, among other things, was to take the Lord's Supper and to give.

Think about it like this. Suppose that you work for a company where you get paid on Friday. Does that mean you get paid on Friday twice a year, once a month, or on special occasions during Christmas? No, it means you get paid every Friday. In the same way, the Christians in the Bible met on the first day of the week to eat the Lord's Supper.

In Spirit

In John 4:24, Jesus explained that those who worship God must worship Him in "spirit and truth." He meant that the outward actions must be what God commands, and the Christian's "spirit" must also take part in the worship. Have you ever finished taking the Lord's Supper and realized that you were so busy thinking about that vacation, the girl or boy sitting beside you, school, or that upcoming soccer game that you did not even stop to think about Jesus and His sacrifice on the cross? You were eating the Lord's Supper in truth, but your "spirit" did not participate.

While it is important to take the Lord's Supper on the first day of the week, that is not too difficult. Many times, the most difficult part of the Lord's Supper is blocking out all the worldly thoughts from your mind and remembering Jesus—thinking about the pain and agony He suffered on the cross for you. The real challenge is to eat the Lord's Supper "in remembrance" of Christ. The next time you put that tiny piece of unleavened bread in your mouth, and sip down that little taste of grape juice, don't forget to remember Jesus' bloody body hanging on that cross saying, "Father, forgive them for they know not what they do."

Chapter 10

God and Money

Kevin loved the 20th of November; for a very good reason. It was his birthday. Today happened to be the 20th of November. He was twelve. For the past eleven years his grandmother sent him a birthday card; but not just a plain old birthday card. She gave him ten dollars—for every year of his life! That meant he was going to get $120 today, if today was like the last eleven years. For two weeks he had been thinking about what he wanted to buy. Radio Shack had the coolest remote control Hummer. It was "only" $89. If he bought that, he would have a little left to buy a new video game for his Playstation. He had also been looking at iPods and MP3 players.

He pulled his clothes on and rushed downstairs. Just as he expected, the birthday card was waiting for him. His dad had it in his hands, tapping it on the rail of the stairs.

"Kevin," said his dad. "I think I've got something you might want."

"Yes, sir. That looks like my birthday card from Grandma."

"It sure is, Son. And if I know your Grandma, this is going to be a lot of money."

"I sure hope so," Kevin answered with excitement.

Kevin's dad handed him the envelope. Kevin took it, opened it, and stared at the cash—6 crisp twenty-dollar bills. It was the most money he had ever been given.

Kevin turned to go back upstairs, but his dad stopped him.

"Kevin, it's time we had a talk."

"About what, dad?"

"It's time we talked about money—and God."

Kevin had never really thought that God and money had much to do with each other. He was interested in what his dad had to say.

"Ok, Dad," said Kevin as he sat down on the couch in the living room.

"Let me ask you a question Son, whose money is that $120 you are holding?"

That seemed like a very silly question. It was his money. His grandmother gave it to him for his birthday. He was surprised his dad asked such an odd question. He looked at his dad and said, "It's my money. Grandma gave it to me."

"Are you sure?" said his Dad.

Kevin thought for a minute. Was he missing something? He didn't owe his dad any of it. Yes, he was confident the money belonged to him.

"Yes, sir. It is my money."

"I thought you might say that, Kevin. But did you know it's not your money?"

"I don't understand" said Kevin in a puzzled voice. "Whose money is it?"

"The Bible tells us that all things, including all the money in the world, belong to God. The money you are holding is really God's money."

Kevin thought about that for a minute, and realized his dad was right.

His dad continued: "God has given you the money to use, but it does not belong to you. God has made you a steward of His money."

"What is a steward?" Kevin asked.

"A steward is someone who takes care of something for another person."

"I think I'm starting to understand," said Kevin. "Like last year when our neighbors left me in charge of feeding and walking their dog. He wasn't my

dog, but I was taking care of him for someone else."

"Exactly, Kevin, I think you are beginning to understand"

Kevin thought for a minute, then he asked his dad, "If this is God's money, what does He want me to do with it?"

"That's a great question. Let's look at what the Bible says."

Kevin's dad picked up his Bible off the coffee table and turned to 1 Corinthians 16:1-2, and read: "Now concerning the collection for the saints, as I have given orders to the churches of Galatia, so you must do also: On the first day of the week let each of you lay something aside, storing up as he may prospe...." "Do you know what that means, Kevin?"

"I think so. That means on Sundays we should give some of our money to God when we meet with the Church."

"Very good, Kevin. You're really picking up on this fast."

"One thing I don't understand, though, Dad. How much should we give? Should we give one dollar? Ten dollars?"

"Great question, Kevin. The verse says each person should give 'as he may prosper.' That means the more a person has, the more he should give. If a person has 100 dollars and gives as he prospers, then he will give more than a person who has 20 dollars."

"So, how much should **I** give?" Kevin said thoughtfully.

"Another great question, Kevin. But it is one you have to answer for yourself. In the Old Testament, the Jews were commanded to give at least 10 percent of their income. That would mean you would give 12 dollars. But we are not under the Old Testament any more."

"Does that mean I could give less than 12 dollars?" said Kevin.

"Well, let's think about that. In 2 Corinthians 9:6-7, the Bible says: 'But this I say: He who sows sparingly will also reap sparingly, and he who sows bountifully will also reap bountifully. So let each one give as he purposes in his heart, not grudgingly or of necessity; for God loves a cheerful giver.'"

"Do you understand these verses, Kevin?"

"Well, it seems like the Bible is saying that God blesses us more if we give more. And we should be happy to give and not be sad about it."

Kevin's dad patted him on the back.

"That is what these verses are saying. Our lives will be better if we learn to give cheerfully. God doesn't demand that we give exactly 10 percent, but He knows that the more we give, the happier we will be. Let me show you another verse. Acts 20:35 says: "And remember the words of the Lord Jesus, that He said, 'It is more blessed to give than to receive.'"

"Kevin, do you understand what Jesus was saying?'"

"Yes, sir. He was saying that getting money and good stuff is fun and exciting. But giving things to others who need them makes a person feel even better than getting things."

Kevin's dad closed his Bible. "I think you understand quite well, Son. I trust that you will be a good steward of God's money."

Kevin went upstairs to his bedroom. After a little thinking, he took a 20-dollar bill out of the card. He decided to give it back to God on Sunday. The other 20-dollar bills went to Radio Shack for the new remote control Hummer. He had fun chasing squirrels with it and jumping ramps in the backyard. And even though he didn't get that new game for his Playstation, he felt great about the way he had taken care of the money God had let him use.

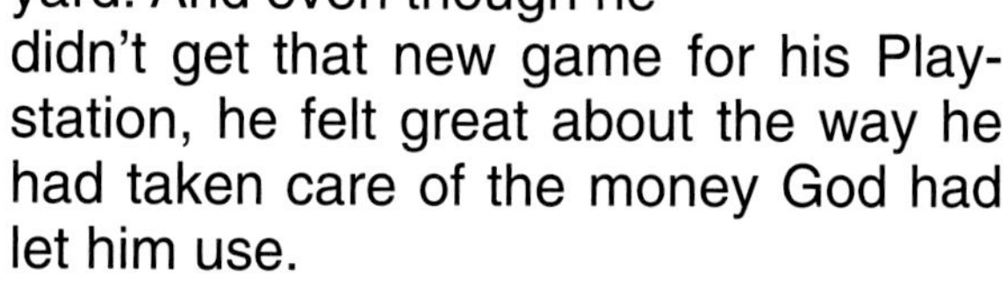

Becoming a good steward is an important part of being a Christian. In fact, in Luke 16:10, Jesus said: "He who is faithful in what is least is faithful also in much; and he who is unjust in what is least is unjust also in much. Therefore if you have not been faithful in the unrighteous riches, who will commit to your trust true riches?"

Jesus was saying that the way you handle money says a lot about your spiritual life. Let's decide to give back to God cheerfully so our lives will be blessed like God wants them to be.

Chapter 11

The Fight to Do Right

Courtney was the most popular girl in the sixth grade. Everybody wanted to be her friend. And everybody wanted her to like them. Some kids would give her the best snacks from their lunches. Other kids would let her boss them around and call them names. Erica was pretty cool too. Lots of the kids liked Erica. But Erica really wanted to be "in" with Courtney and her friends. She wanted Courtney to think she was cool. One day Courtney saw Erica talking to the new girl at school. Courtney and her friends sat down by Erica at lunch.

"Saw you talking to the new girl," Courtney said.

"Yeah, her name's Matilda. She's from Illinois."

"You don't like her do you?" Courtney said menacingly, "She's such a nerd."

Erica was in a tight spot. She really did like Matilda and she wanted to tell Courtney the truth. But she knew Courtney and her friends would make fun of her and laugh at her. She would certainly lose some "cool points" if she stuck up for Matilda. She wanted to tell the truth, but she also wanted to fit in. So Erica decided to....

What? What did Erica decide to do? Or maybe a better question is what did you decide to do? When you were tempted to do something you knew was wrong just so you would fit in, did you do it? Or did you stand up for what you knew was right, even though your "friends" thought it was "uncool" and called you names? The truth is we've all been there. We have all been tempted.

What is Temptation?

What is temptation? That's an easy question. Temptation is when you have a desire to do something that is against God's will. If you want that new shirt really badly, but don't have any money, you might be tempted to steal it. If you want kids at school to like you, you might be tempted to say curse words to fit in with them. If you run through the house and break your mom's antique clock, you might be tempted to lie so that you don't get in trouble. We are tempted when we desire something that would make us disobey God. The book of James says: "Each one is tempted when he is drawn away by his own desires" (James 1:14).

We need to know something very important about temptation. It is not wrong to be tempted. Even Jesus was tempted. The Bible says that Jesus was tempted in all the same ways that other humans are tempted (read Hebrews 4:15). But Jesus was different from the rest of us in a very important way. Even though he was often tempted to sin, He never did. He fought temptation and always won.

Fighting temptation is like exercise. If you do push-ups every night, your arm muscles will get stronger. You will be able to do more and more push-ups the more nights you do them. But if you

stop doing push-ups after the first night because they are hard or because they make your arms sore, you won't get any stronger. In a similar way, if we "endure" (or fight through) temptation we will get spiritually stronger.

How Do We Fight Temptation?

When we are tempted, the devil is trying to entice us to disobey God—just like he did to Jesus. In Matthew chapter 4, we read that the devil tried three times to tempt Jesus to sin. But every time Jesus was tempted by the devil, He answered the devil by saying, "It is written," and then Jesus quoted a Scripture. Jesus used the Bible to defeat Satan and temptation. We can do the same thing today. In Ephesians 6:17, we are told that the Word of God is the sword of the spirit. It is the weapon we use to fight the devil. When he tempts us to lie to our friends, we can fight back with our "sword" by saying, "The Bible says we should not lie, but tell the truth" (read Ephesians 4:25). When Satan tempts us to be mean to someone at school, we can jab back at him by quoting the Golden Rule: "Do unto others as you would have them do to you" (read Matthew 7:12).

In order to fight temptation with the sword of the spirit (God's Word) you have to **know God's Word**. You don't have to carry a Bible around and read it every time you are tempted. But it is important to know what is says. King David, in the Old Testament, once said to God: "Your word have I hidden in my heart, that I might not sin against You" (Psalm 119:9). When we read and study God's Word, we hide it in our hearts. Then when Satan tries to tempt us to do wrong, we can defeat him by remembering God's Word.

What If We Sin?

Being baptized is a wonderful thing. When you are baptized, the blood of Jesus forgives all your sins—all those times you lost the fight with temptation. But some people have the wrong idea about baptism. They think that after they are baptized, they will never sin again. In fact, some people don't want to get baptized, because they know that they will not be able to live perfect lives. The truth is, everybody sins, even after they are baptized. Becoming a Christian doesn't mean you will never sin again. In 1 John, the Bible says: "My little children, these things I write to you that you may not sin." That is clear. John was writing so we wouldn't sin. But then he says, "And if anyone sins, we have an Advocate with the Father, Jesus Christ the righteous" (1 John 2:1).

God knew we would sin, even after we became Christians, so He sent Jesus to be our advocate. What is an advocate? It is like a lawyer; someone who pleads our case to God; someone who stands up for us and gets us "off the hook." Since Jesus was tempted just like us, He knows how to talk to God for us. In fact, when we sin, we just have to confess our sins to God, repent and decide to stop sinning, and God will forgive us (read 1 John 1:9). It doesn't matter how many times we sin, God **will always forgive** us if we follow those steps.

The more we fight temptation, the stronger we will get. God's word is the perfect weapon for defeating the devil. Sometimes we will lose the fight and sin, but Jesus talks to God for us, and our sins are forgiven when we confess and repent. The next time you are tempted to lie, cheat, steal, or say a bad word, remember how Jesus was tempted but never sinned. His example can help us defeat temptation.

Chapter 12

Telling Others the Good News

Thomas and his family had been planning a trip to Disney World for months. They had their plane tickets, hotel reservations, park tickets, and maps and schedules to help them do everything they wanted to do. Thomas had been anxiously looking forward to their trip for a long time. He had never been to Disney World, but he had researched it on the Web and it looked like it was going to be fun. Jimmy, his friend at school, went last year and told him about all the cool rides and the fireworks that are shot off every night. Thomas was excited. Some nights he could hardly go to sleep because he was thinking about the trip.

Because of his excitement, he told everyone about the trip. When Ms. Madison, his teacher, asked if anyone was doing anything fun over the summer, Thomas was the first to raise his hand and tell about his plans. In conversations with his friends, he would slip it in. Like when Jimmy asked him to come to his birthday party, Thomas said: "Can't make it, man, I'll be at Disney World." Thomas **had** to inform his Boy Scout troop that he wouldn't be able to do anything with them the week of his trip. He could even handle not making baseball All-Stars this year, "because," he told some of the kids on his team, "I'd probably have to miss the important game to go to Disney World anyway." Thomas was excited about his trip and everyone knew it, because he looked for every opportunity to tell people about it.

Have you ever been so excited about something that you wanted to tell others about it? Sure you have. Maybe it was a trip, some new gadget you got for Christmas, or some famous person you met. What is the most exciting thing that has ever happened to you?

If you think hard, you will probably realize that becoming a Christian is the most exciting thing that has ever happened to you. When you were baptized, the Lord added you to His Church. All your sins were washed away. And God promised you a home in heaven, a place much more exciting and enjoyable than any place here on Earth. So what are you going to do about your exciting new life with Jesus? Don't you want other people to feel as happy and excited about their spiritual lives as you do about yours? Don't you want others to know how they can have their sins washed away and how God will give them a home in heaven, too? Absolutely!

But did you know that the only way that others will hear about Jesus and heaven is if someone tells them. That's right. It is every Christian's job to tell others about Jesus and His plan to save them. Just before Jesus went back to heaven to be with God, He gave His disciples a very important command. He said to them: "Go therefore and make disciples of all the nations, baptizing them in the name of the Father and the Son and of the Holy Spirit, teaching them to observe all things that I have commanded you; and lo, I am with you always, even to the end of the age" (Matthew 28:19-20).

Jesus told His disciples to go and teach all over the world. The entire book of Acts (in the New Testament) is the story of His disciples obeying His command and teaching people about Jesus. Peter preached the story of Jesus to the Jews in Acts chapter 2. In Acts chapter 8, the Bible tells about a man named Philip who told a wealthy treasurer about

Jesus. The wealthy treasurer believed in Jesus and was baptized, exactly like you were (read Acts 8:38-39). Sometimes the disciples of Jesus suffered terrible things because they told others about Jesus. Some of Jesus' disciples were killed, others were beaten and thrown into prison. But that didn't stop them. They knew that God wanted everybody to have a chance to hear about Jesus and heaven. So they kept telling others the good news, even though it sometimes cost them their lives.

The book of Acts also tells about the amazing apostle Paul. He had been a wicked man who persecuted the Church and tried to hurt Christians. But when he met Jesus and became a Christian, his life changed forever. He went on three missionary trips to tell thousands of people about Jesus. He preached in cities like Athens, Corinth, Philippi, and Ephesus. Many of the books of the New Testament—like Ephesians and Philippians—are letters he wrote to the people who became Christians in those cities. One time, Paul told a young man named Timothy to "preach the word." He wanted Timothy to tell others the good news about Jesus just like Paul had been telling them.

But teaching others about Jesus and the Bible is not something just for apostles or preachers. God wants all Christians to follow the examples of Jesus and His apostles. He wants **you** to tell others about Jesus and how to be saved. New Christians sometimes think that they are too young to tell others about how to be saved. Others think they just don't know enough about the Bible to help others understand. But the truth is, you are never too young to tell others about Christ, and you don't have to know every thing about the Bible. You just need to be excited about Jesus and be willing to help others find answers in the Bible.

You don't have to go on long missionary trips like Paul did. And you don't have to walk from village to village like Jesus did. You can tell your friends at school about Jesus. Maybe you could tell your cousins about what the

Bible says about becoming a Christian and going to heaven. There are many different ways to spread the good news. You could get some tracts at the church building and mail them to people you have met. Or you could give your friends books that you think might help them.

The story of Jesus and His plan to save humans is called the Gospel. The word "Gospel" means "good news." The Gospel is the best news in the entire world! It is the only news that can save people from their sins and help them go to heaven. But people who do not know about Jesus will not be saved unless someone tells them the good news—someone like you. The Bible says that people who tell others about the Gospel are people who "bring glad tidings of good things." In a way, it's like telling other people about a great trip you are going on to see Jesus and live with Him in heaven. But the wonderful thing about this trip is that everyone is invited. So let's all make sure we are doing our part to spread the good news, and invite as many people as we can to come on our exciting trip to heaven.

Chapter 13

What Do I Get Out of It?

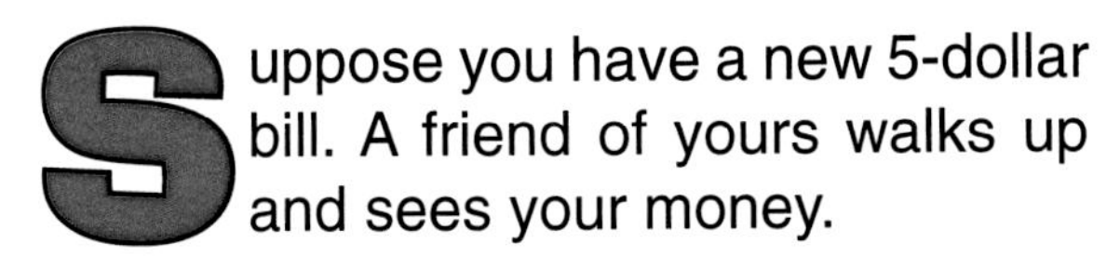

Suppose you have a new 5-dollar bill. A friend of yours walks up and sees your money.

"Hey. What's that for?"

"Lunch money," you reply.

"Can I see it?" says your friend.

"Sure."

You hand him the money. He takes it from you and looks it over. You can tell he is thinking hard. His face shows you that he has come up with a plan.

"I was thinking," says he, "This piece of money is only one bill. Do you want to trade something for it?"

You're not totally against trading, especially if he's got something good, so you ask, "What do you have in mind?"

"Well, let me show you."

He pulls 3 bills from his pocket. They are 1-dollar bills. He counts them slowly in front of you. Then he looks at your bill.

"You know, you only have one bill. I have three. I'll give you three bills for your one."

You can count, and you can see that he does have 2 more bills than you. But are you going to trade with him? No way! Why not? Because his 3 1-dollar bills are not worth as much as your 5-dollar bill.

So what does that have to do with being a Christian? Simple. God wants you to obey Him. In return for your obedience, He has offered to "trade" you some things. Every person must decide if they want to accept God's offer. So, what does God offer you? That is a good question. Let's look at just a few of the things God offers if you obey Him.

Peace

Have you ever had the feeling that things were not going to turn out right? Maybe you felt like you were going to lose someone you loved? Maybe you worried that you were going to get really sick. Or maybe you felt like God was mad at you and you were not going to heaven. God tells you that if you obey Him, He can help take away those kinds of feelings. He promises to give you peace. He says that if you obey Him and pray to Him, then He will give you "the peace of God, which surpasses all understanding." He also says that this peace will "guard your hearts and minds through Christ Jesus" (read Philippians 4:7). That means God will help you to feel good about your life. He will help you stop worrying about losing someone or getting sick. He will help you understand that He is not angry with you. It doesn't mean bad things will never happen to you. It just means that God will help you deal with them. Many bad things happened to righteous people in the Bible. But they trusted God. Because they trusted them, He gave them peace and helped them to understand that all things work together for good to those who love God (Romans 8:28).

Forgiveness

Everybody sins. Sin often makes a person's conscience hurt. When your conscience hurts, you feel bad. In fact, it is one of the worst feelings in the world. Think back to a time when you did something wrong. Maybe you stole something. You might have cheated on a test. Or perhaps you looked at something on the Internet you should not have. Do you remember how it felt when you realized you did wrong? You knew you were guilty of sin. It was almost like a little voice in your head kept reminding

you how bad you had been. God gave you a conscience for a reason. When you do wrong, He wants you to feel bad about yourself. He wants you to look for a way to feel better. He wants you to find Him. He is the only one Who has a cure for sin. Only God can forgive your sins. When you were baptized, God washed your sins away with Jesus' blood. He promises to continue to forgive you as long as you repent and ask for forgiveness. But He is the only One who can forgive your sins. When people don't obey God, they live their lives in sin. They never get forgiveness. Forgiveness is a wonderful gift that God offers to all who obey Him.

Eternal Life

One of the saddest things about life is death. Plants die. Pets die. People die. Everybody dies. Our grandparents die. One day our parents will die. And when we really stop and think, we realize that we will die, too. It seems sad to think like that. It is scary and sad to think that our parents, or brothers and sisters, will one day die. But the Bible says that all those who obey God will live forever in heaven. John says: "And this is the promise that He has promised us—eternal life" (1 John 2:25). That means that God will let us live forever and ever. We will never die. We do not need to be scared of death, because death does not have any power over those who obey God.

Have you ever been separated from your parents for a little while? Maybe

your parents went on a weekend trip and left you with relatives or friends. You might have been a little sad at first. But you got over that quickly, because you knew you would see them again soon. When Christians leave this physical life, they are not gone forever. They are just separated from other Christians for a little while. Even though it is sad when they leave this world, we can know that we will see them again. The Old Testament contains a great story about King David. He had a baby son who became very sick. This son died soon after he was born. David was sad, but he knew that he would see his son again. In fact, David said that one day he would be able to be with his son again (2 Samuel 12:23). Only God can offer us eternal life.

No Pain, Sickness, or Crying

Breaking your arm is no fun. It really hurts. In fact, lots of things hurt. Getting shots at the dentist can be quite painful. Falling on concrete and skinning your elbows and knees is tough. Getting burned by a stove can be agonizing. All of us have been hurt. We have cried because of the pain we felt. Wouldn't it be great if there was a place where pain did not exist? There is such a place. God created heaven for Christians. In heaven, "God will wipe away every tear from their eyes; there shall be no more death, nor sorrow, nor crying; and there shall be no more pain" (Revelation 21:4). God Himself will take care of us. He will take away everything that causes us pain. Heaven will be the perfect home. We will live with God, Jesus, angels, and all those people who have obeyed God. We will live perfectly happy lives.

Do We Have a Deal?

After looking at a few of the things God offers, do you think you want to make a deal with Him? Do you want to give Him your life in exchange for peace, eternal life, and a perfectly happy existence in heaven? The truth is, God offers us much more than our lives are worth. But He loves us and wants us to be happy. Sadly, some people refuse God's offer. Those people make a very bad decision. When we learn what God offers us, it makes obeying Him much more rewarding.

Afterword

Chris' body ached all over. His knees throbbed with pain. His body was soaked with sweat. He could hardly concentrate on anything. He stared down at his feet. They seemed to belong to someone else. He saw them going, one in front of the other, but he could barely believe he was making them move. He and his dad had run more than twenty-five miles. They had been running for over four hours. The water stations along the course kept him hydrated, but his muscles were rebelling. They didn't want to go another step. Then suddenly, Chris heard his dad say: "Hey, Chris. Do you see it? There it is—the finish line." He raised his head to look.

It was one of the most wonderful sights he had ever seen in his life. Hundreds of people lined the street, cheering the runners on. A loud speaker announced the numbers of the finishers as they crossed the finish line. If Chris could just push himself a little further. That line meant victory. The satisfaction of knowing he completed a marathon. And rest—he could see himself lying on the cool grass after gulping down a huge Gatorade. His body felt a little lighter and his muscles ached less. He began to pick up his pace. Just a few short strides left. The crowd was cheering for him. "You can do it," they yelled. "Almost there, keep running." The encouraging words helped Chris pick up the pace a little more. Just 100 yards left. Now 50 yards. A few more feet. Yes! He did it. He finished the race. He pushed his body farther than it had ever been. And he didn't quit. He was a marathon runner.

Chris finished his race, will you finish yours. Remember, being a Christian is like running a race. It is not a sprint to see who will cross the finish line first. It is a marathon that takes the rest of your life to run. And it does not matter if other people cross the line before you. As long as you stay in the race, and remain a faithful Christian, you are a champion. It is sad, but many people start the Christian race, and quit along the way. They go back to their worldly friends and the sinful lives they were living before they became Christians. They turn their back on God, their Christian family, and heaven. This saddens God, because He wants all people to be saved. In the book of Revelation, Jesus spoke to the church in Smyrna. He told them that they were going to be tempted by Satan and have very difficult lives for a while. But Jesus told them: "Be faithful until death, and I will give you the crown of life" (Revelation 2:10). You have made the decision to be a Christian. Will you be a faithful Christian for the rest of your life so that you can live in heaven with God forever? "You can do it." "Keep running." "It will all be worth it."